How is it Made?
Paper

Wendy Blaxland

MACMILLAN
LIBRARY

First published in 2008 by
MACMILLAN EDUCATION AUSTRALIA PTY LTD
15–19 Claremont Street, South Yarra 3141

Visit our website at www.macmillan.com.au or go directly to www.macmillanlibrary.com.au

Associated companies and representatives throughout the world.

National Library of Australia
Cataloguing-in-Publication data

Blaxland, Wendy, 1949-
    Paper / author, Wendy Blaxland.
    South Yarra, Vic. : Macmillan Education, 2008.
    ISBN: 978 1 4202 6411 1 (hbk.)
    Blaxland, Wendy, 1949- How are they made?
    Includes index.
    For primary school age.
    Paper--Juvenile literature.
    Papermaking--Juvenile literature.
    Waste paper--Recycling--Juvenile literature.
676

Edited by Anna Fern
Cover design, text design and page layout by Cristina Neri, Canary Graphic Design
Photo research by Legend Images
Map by Damien Demaj, DEMAP; modified by Cristina Neri, Canary Graphic Design

Printed in China

Acknowledgements

The author would like to thank the following people for their expert advice: Scot Alexander, Wikipedia; Tony Ashton of the
Australasian Paper Industry Association; Alan Cole, Chairman, Museum of Writing, University of London; and Ralph Coghill,
Executive Director of APPITA.

The author and the publisher are grateful to the following for permission to reproduce copyright material:

Front cover photograph: Blue origami bird (crane) © Olga Shelego/iStockphoto; paper airplane © Melanie Kintz/iStock-
photo; roll of white paper towels © omer sukru goksu/iStockphoto; Mexican donkey piñata © Valerie Loiseleux/iStockphoto.
Images repeated throughout title.

Photos courtesy of:
The Art Archive/Private Collection/Marc Charmet, **7**; Australasian Paper Industry Association Ltd., **20**, **21** (top), **22** (bottom),
23; Eyewire/Joseph Sohm-Visions of America, **14**; The Bridgeman Art Library/Getty Images, **4** (bottom right); China Photos/
Getty Images, **27** (top); Louie Psihoyos/Getty Images, **26**; Lee Balterman/Time Life Pictures/Getty Images, **19** (right); iStock-
photo, **11** (top); © nicholas belton/iStockphoto, **10**; © Spauln/iStockphoto, **4**, **5** (bottom right); Jupiterimages/Corbis Royalty
Free, **30** (bottom); PaperChase, www.paperchase.com.au, **25**; Photodisc, **5** (top); Photodisc/The Palma Collection, **24**; Photo-
disc/Jack Star/PhotoLink, **5** (bottom left); © Gabe Palmer/Alamy/Photolibrary, **18** (bottom); © PhotoAlto/Alamy/Photolibrary, **8**;
Photolibrary/Photo Researchers/David R Frazier, **16** (bottom), **17**; Photos.com, **4** (bottom left); Robert C. Williams American
Museum of Papermaking, Institute of Paper Science and Technology, Georgia Tech, **9** (bottom); © Sybille Yates/Shutterstock,
29; Willmott Forests Limited, via Tony Wood, **28** (bottom).

Headshot illustrations accompanying textboxes throughout title © Russell Tate/iStockphoto.

Text 'Qualities of handmade paper', **27**, from http://www.hqpapermaker.com/paper-history/. HQ PaperMaker™ is a
trademark of HQ Group Company Limited. © Copyright 2004 HQ Group Co. Ltd.

While every care has been taken to trace and acknowledge copyright, the publisher tenders their apologies for any
accidental infringement where copyright has proved untraceable. Where the attempt has been unsuccessful,
the publisher welcomes information that would redress the situation.

Contents

Glossary words

When a word is printed in **bold**, you can look up its meaning in the Glossary on page 31.

From raw materials to products

Everything we use is made from raw materials from the Earth. These are called natural resources. People take natural resources and make them into useful products.

Paper

Paper is a material usually made in thin, **flexible** sheets. It is especially useful for writing and printing on.

The main raw material used to make paper is wood from trees. The wood is chopped into woodchips and made into pulp. The wood pulp is also mixed with small amounts of clay and **chalk**, which are dug from the ground, and other chemicals.

Although most of our paper is made from wood pulp, other plants can be used, including bamboo, sugarcane, wheat straw and grasses.

Question & Answer

Where does the word 'paper' come from?

The word paper comes from the Greek term for papyrus, the ancient Egyptian writing material. This marsh grass was peeled and sliced into strips. Then it was pounded and smoothed into flat sheets.

Dictionaries are often printed on thin paper, because there are so many pages.

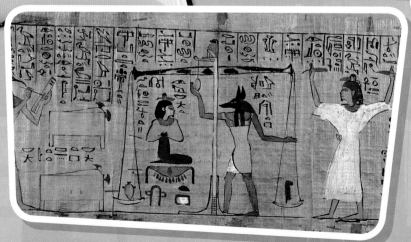

This ancient Egyptian account of a funeral is written on a sheet of papyrus.

Guess What!

A stack of logs 1.2 metres tall, 1.2 metres deep and 2.4 metres long can be used to make 30 rocking chairs, 900 books weighing 500 grams each, 10 000 one-litre milk containers or 7 500 000 toothpicks.

Why do we need paper?

Paper is mainly used for writing and storing information. Before paper was invented, people wrote on cave walls, on clay tablets and on stone. Unlike these early materials, paper is light and thin, so it can be rolled, folded or cut and made into books. Books made of paper can store much more information than other ways of writing and are more easily transported.

Now we use paper in a wide range of ways. This includes books, cardboard cartons, paper money, birth certificates, stamps and nappies. There are many different types of paper, in different thicknesses, textures, colours and sizes that suit different purposes.

Although paperless electronic communication is becoming more important, paper still plays a vital part in the way our world operates.

Tissues are made from layers of thin paper, so they are soft and absorbent.

Newspapers are printed on cheap, low-quality paper because they are not meant to last.

The history of paper

Paper is one of the most important human inventions. Paper makes it possible to record thoughts and ideas easily and communicate them to people in other places and other times. The ancient Egyptian, Chinese and Central American Mayan cultures all invented paper-making independently. Writing on paper helped these cultures organise large empires. In the 1800s, machines to make pulp and paper were invented. This allowed cheap, wood-based paper to be made. Together with mass-produced pencils, cheap paper meant that books, newspapers and education became widely available.

Question & Answer

What are parchment and vellum?

Parchment is made from animal skins. Used since Roman times, it was the main writing material in Europe for important material like Bibles before the 1500s. Parchment was generally made of calfskin or sheepskin. It is estimated that writing a single Bible by hand on parchment needed the skins of 300 sheep. Vellum is the best quality parchment.

Paper through the ages

500 CE The Mayan civilisation in Central America develops paper. It is used widely through this area until the Spanish conquest in the 1500s.

610 Paper-making spreads from Korea to Japan where **fibres** from the mulberry tree are used.

751 Muslim Arabs in central Asia defeat Chinese troops and use prisoners who are papermakers to start a paper mill in Samarkand (in modern-day Uzbekistan).

3000 BCE Papyrus is made into paper in Egypt.

104 CE Tsai-Lun makes paper in China. The Chinese guard their paper-making secrets carefully.

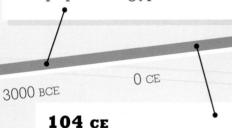

604 The techniques of Chinese paper-making are introduced to Korea.

900s The Arabs improve paper-making techniques and spread the knowledge throughout the Muslim world, including Spain. They use plant fibres, such as hemp and flax, and **linen** rags.

3000 BCE   0 CE   250 CE   500 CE   750 CE   1000

This illustration shows the workshop of Johannes Gutenberg, whose invention of the printing press made it possible for books to become widely available.

1100s Christians drive the Muslim Arabs from Spain and take over the Arab paper mills.

1200s Mills appear in Italy. Italian paper-makers improve the process, using water mills to drive their machines, which include stamping mills to produce finer pulp, and wire mesh driers.

1500s Four experienced men can make up to 4500 sheets of paper in a 13-hour working day.

1630 The first grocery paper bags are used in Europe.

2000s The rise of electronic communication means less demand for some paper, but greater demand for A4 paper to print on.

1500 CE 1600 CE 1700 CE 1800 CE 1900 CE 2000 CE

1120 The first paper mill in Europe is built at Xavia (now Valencia) in Spain.

1450s Johannes Gutenberg develops the **printing press** in Germany. Printing creates a great demand for paper.

1700s A machine invented by the Fourdrinier brothers in England produces paper in a continuous sheet.

1860 All parts of paper-making are now done by machine.

1838 The first wood-pulp paper in Europe is made by Saxon Keller.

What is paper made from?

Paper is mostly made from wood pulp. It also contains a surprising number of other materials, including clay, chalk, dye, inks, starch and sometimes even plastic. Many other decorative materials, called inclusions, can also be added during paper-making.

High quality paper may have a watermark to identify who made the paper, and when or where. The watermark is visible when the paper is held against a light. Watermarks are sometimes used on banknotes or documents to help prevent faking. The paper can also be **embossed**, or have a pattern pressed into it, after it has been made.

embossing

deckle edge

inclusions

The uneven 'deckle' edge of this paper shows that it has been handmade.

Materials

Many different raw materials are used to make paper. As with the making of all products, energy is also used to run the machines that help harvest the trees, mine the minerals and turn wood pulp into paper.

Materials used to make paper

Material	Purpose and qualities
Wood pulp (cellulose fibres)	Gives the body of the paper structure and strength. Makes the paper able to absorb water.
Linen and cotton (cellulose fibres)	Gives body of the paper structure and strength. Makes the paper able to last a long time.
Kaolin or chalk	Gives paper **opacity** and a smooth, white surface for writing on.
Dye	Colours the paper.
Inks	Decorate the surface of the paper.
Plastic	Gives the surface of paper a waterproof, glossy finish.
Leaves, metal and other inclusions	Gives the paper a decorative texture and appearance.
Chlorine	Bleaches paper white.
Chemicals (such as starch)	Depending on the sort of paper, different chemicals may be used to brighten, soften, stiffen or strengthen the paper, or make it more or less absorbent.

Some watermarks are works of art in their own right.

9

Paper design

Paper is used for writing and drawing, and to make a huge range of objects. Depending on its purpose, designers make paper with different qualities using different materials.

Paper can be made in different weights and thicknesses. It can be lightweight, flexible and easy to cut, or it can be made stiff, heavy and hard to cut, like cardboard. Some papers need to be soft, absorbent and strong, such as paper tissues, or quick to break up, such as toilet paper.

Paper can be made to absorb colouring, such as special watercolour artists' paper. It may also be waterproofed with a coating of plastic or wax and used to keep food fresh.

Paper can be made with different textures and patterned surfaces, from smooth paper for writing to rough or embossed papers for craft and wrapping presents. Paper comes in a wide variety of colours.

Stamps are tiny works of art printed on paper with adhesive on the back.

Intricate origami designs can be created by simply folding a sheet of paper, without any gluing or cutting.

Paper for making models

Paper is also used to help design other objects, such as dressmaking patterns and scale models of buildings or theatrical set designs. Paper is ideal for models because it is cheap, and easy to work with and change. This paper can be fine, such as dressmaking tissue, or sturdy, such as paper for models.

Question & Answer

What is origami?

Origami is the ancient Japanese art of paper folding. It was first mentioned in the 300s CE. Traditional origami includes figures such as orizuru (a folded paper crane), a symbol of hope and peace.

From wood to paper

The process of making everyday objects such as paper from raw materials involves a large number of steps. In the first stage, trees are cut down. Next, they are chopped more finely into woodchips and then pulped to extract the cellulose fibres that make paper. In the second stage, the wood pulp, along with recycled paper, clay, dyes and other chemicals, is made into paper by machines, using water and electricity. The final stage involves drying the paper and finishing it. Paper is finished differently for different purposes, cut to the right size and often coated with clays and inks.

Stage 2

Stage 1: Making pulp from wood

Trees are harvested.

↓

Next, the logs are cut into woodchips.

↓

The woodchips are then made into pulp by being ground up by machines or cooked with chemicals.

Stage 3: Drying and finishing paper

The paper is squeezed on rollers to remove most of the water.

Then it is coated with materials such as clay to give the desired surface.

Next, the paper is passed through polished metal rollers to make it smooth.

Then the paper is wound onto huge rolls.

Finally, it is cut into smaller rolls or into sheets.

Making paper from pulp

The wood pulp is first washed and usually bleached whiter.

The pulp is then blended with substances to give the paper different qualities, such as colour, softness, stiffness or waterproofing.

Next, the pulp **slurry** is placed on a wire screen.

Then the water is drained from the pulp and the fibres mat or join together to make a sheet of paper.

Question & Answer

What is mummy paper?

Paper can be made from recycled linen and cotton rags. When rags were scarce in the 1800s, even the linen wrapped around ancient Egyptian mummies was used. **Imported** in shiploads into the United States, this linen was made into brown wrapping paper.

Raw materials for paper

Paper consists of a mat of cellulose fibres. Cellulose is found in most plants, including trees. Wood provides the major raw material for paper. This generally comes from **softwood trees**, such as spruce and pine, which have long, soft fibres. Some **hardwood trees**, such as fast-growing eucalyptus and birch, are also used. Paper can also be made from straw and bamboo.

Other raw materials for making paper include kaolin, clay or chalk mined from the ground, dyes, inks, chlorine to bleach the paper white, and other chemicals for a range of purposes. Plastic is used to coat some papers. The plastic is made in **petrochemical factories** from oil, which is pumped from underground wells.

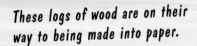
These logs of wood are on their way to being made into paper.

Guess What!

In the past, even old canvas sails were used to make paper. Other unusual paper-making materials included banana leaves, seaweed and even bison and kangaroo dung.

Centres for paper production

The paper industry produces over 300 million tonnes of paper a year, worth over US $500 billion ($500 000 000 000). One-third of this paper comes from the United States, where the paper industry is a major employer. The United States and Canada produce 40 per cent of the world's paper pulp. The United States and China together use over 40 per cent of the pulp.

The United States and China make almost 40 per cent of the world's paper and **paperboard**. Germany, Canada and the United States **export** the most paper.

Key

- ✪ Important wood-growing countries
- ◆ Important pulp-manufacturing countries
- ✈ Important paper-manufacturing countries

Guess What!

Starch is an important ingredient in paper. In Europe the starch usually comes from potato, in Asia from tapioca, in America from corn and in Australia from wheat.

This map shows countries that are important to the production of paper.

15

From wood to paper
Stage 1: Making pulp from wood

The basic raw material for paper is wood. Many paper firms own and manage **timber plantations** because they need a lot of wood.

After the timber is harvested, the logs pass through a machine that removes the bark. Then the logs travel through machines called chippers, with spinning blades that cut the wood into 2.5 centimetre chips.

The next step, called 'pulping', is to break the woodchips down into fibres. Wood consists of fibres joined by a chemical called lignin. The lignin must be broken down to separate the fibres. This is done either by grinding the woodchips in machines or with chemicals.

Mechanical pulping

In mechanical pulping, large machines called refiners grind the woodchips into pulp. The woodchips may be softened with steam before grinding. Mechanical pulping makes a weak paper that is suitable for newsprint and paperboard. This paper turns yellow with age because the lignin stays in the pulp. About 95 per cent of the wood, however, is turned into paper.

Logs are cut into woodchips in a chipper.

Woodchips are mixed with water and chemicals and broken down into pulp.

Chemical pulping

Chemical pulping removes the lignin and produces stronger paper. Woodchips are cooked with chemicals in an enormous vat to dissolve the lignin. Only 40 to 50 per cent of the original wood remains. Paper made from chemical pulp is stronger and brighter but more expensive than mechanically made pulp.

Using water

The raw materials for paper pulp are mixed with up to 100 times their weight in water. Modern paper mills have equipment that can clean the water and reuse it many times.

Stage 2: Making paper from pulp

Paper-making today relies on huge, costly machines, up to 13 metres wide, 100 metres long and over two storeys high, costing $500 million. They can produce over 60 kilometres of paper an hour and are run by computers using sensors to control the process. This means that they need very few workers to run them. Paper-making machines vary in size and speed, but all perform the same basic process.

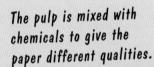

The pulp is mixed with chemicals to give the paper different qualities.

Preparing the pulp

The pulp is washed and usually bleached to whiten it. Bleaching used to be done with chlorine, a poisonous chemical. Now, alternatives such as chlorine dioxide, oxygen, ozone and hydrogen peroxide are mostly used.

The pulp may then be blended with:

* dyes to colour the paper
* minerals to change the way the paper looks
* materials to 'size' or coat the paper to reduce the way it takes up ink and water
* brightening chemicals and softening agents
* starch to strengthen the paper or help bond layers of cardboard
* plastics to make the paper waterproof.

The pulp is sprayed onto a wire screen to form a sheet of paper.

Forming the paper

The prepared pulp slush is fed into a part of the paper-making machine called the head box. The head box pumps the slush onto a moving wire screen to be formed into a paper sheet or web. The water then drains and is sucked away.

Paper is formed in a continuous ribbon, which is wound on rollers to become one long strip.

Guess What!

Fine photocopying paper is made out of hardwood pulp, reinforced with stronger and more expensive softwood pulp.

Stage 3: Drying and finishing paper

The wet paper web is squeezed between large rollers to remove most of the water, which is absorbed by a material called felt. The rollers also make the paper smooth and evenly thick.

Can dryers remove the remaining water by a combination of heat and air flow. The dryers are cylinder-shaped, like cans, and are heated by steam.

Next, the waste water is cleaned and **filtered**. Then it is recycled or released and the waste removed and burnt as fuel.

The rollers on paper-making machines remove water and make the paper smooth.

BELOIT

BELOIT

Question & Answer

When was toilet paper invented?

In 1391, the Chinese Emperor's household produced toilet paper. In the 1880s, the first rolls of tear-off toilet paper were produced.

The finishing process

The paper may be coated with clay-based substances, called sizing, to control how much water and ink are absorbed. It is then dried again.

Next, the paper is sent through a machine called a calender. This presses and smoothes the surface of the paper by passing it through a series of polished metal rollers.

The finished paper is wound into large rolls, which can be up to 13 metres wide and weigh almost 25 tonnes. The paper is then cut by a slitter into smaller rolls that are easy to handle.

Finally, the paper is made into sheets by slitting up to eight rolls at a time. The paper is tested to check it is evenly coloured and surfaced, and that it resists water and holds ink. Sheets must be square and accurate in length to within 1 millimetre. They must also be free of dust to print without leaving blank spots.

When it is dry and finished, paper is wound into huge rolls weighing many tonnes.

Packaging and distribution

Products are packaged to protect them while they are being transported. Packaging also displays the maker's brand and makes products look attractive when they are sold.

Reels or sheets of paper are wrapped in plastic or paper. Small reels may be packed together. Sheets are automatically packed in reams of 500. Then they are loaded onto **pallets** and stored in a warehouse. In the warehouse, the amount of moisture in the air is controlled to keep the paper dry.

Some plain paper, such as photocopy paper, is packed into small packages. These are packed into large boxes and pallet-loads and sent in large quantities to **wholesalers** by truck or rail, or overseas by ship.

Paper must be neatly stored to prevent it being damaged.

Guess What!

Some warehouses are run entirely by robots, which use scanners to find pallets and reels by their barcodes. These warehouses do not even need lights.

22

Rolls of brown paper are stored in a warehouse before being made into other products, such as cardboard boxes.

Distribution

If paper is to be sold as paper, wholesalers pass it to **distributors** who send it to shops and supermarkets. Most paper, however, is used for printing or to make other products, so it is usually shipped to other companies.

Paper made into other products

Making products from paper may take just a few steps. To make a simple product such as a newspaper, reels of paper are printed, cut and distributed to shops to be sold.

Other paper products may involve a number of more complicated steps. Corrugated cardboard is made from layers of stiff, strong paper that is crinkled and glued in a machine called a corrugator. The corrugator is as long as a football field and 4 to 5 metres wide. The continuous cardboard sheet is cut into pieces. The pieces are then printed, cut and glued into boxes. Next, the boxes are sent to other companies, such as toy **manufacturers** and food processors, to be used as packaging for other products.

Marketing and advertising are used to promote and sell products.

Marketing

Paper is used widely in different ways, from paper for writing, to objects such as paper towels and packaging such as boxes. Paper may also be part of other material, such as plasterboard. Paper is sold to all these different markets in different ways.

Plain paper is marketed according to qualities such as size, weight, colour and cost. Special paper, such as wrapping paper, is often marketed by the way it looks and feels.

Paper is sold to manufacturers according to its different qualities, its availability and price. Packagers need sturdy paper. Tissue manufacturers need soft paper.

Guess What!

Flat paper dolls with separate paper clothing were used in the mid 1770s as French fashion dolls for adults. Now, however, paper dolls are mainly toys for children. The first was Little Fanny, made in 1810 in London, England.

Sets of paper dolls with different clothes to wear were cheap toys in the 1800s.

Advertising

Paper is usually advertised to individual customers with other related goods, such as pens. At back-to-school time, shops send out sales brochures advertising paper and other stationery.

Traditionally, manufacturers buying paper go to trade shows where paper is displayed. They can now also buy online. Sales representatives will also travel to manufacturers to sell paper to them.

Some companies advertise 'green' paper made from recycled material or in environmentally friendly ways.

Electronic communication now competes with print media, such as newspapers, magazines and books. The Internet has also attracted money for advertising and investment away from the paper industry, which is also facing increased costs for energy, production, transport and distribution.

Cheap computers, however, have led to an increased number of home offices, which has created a huge demand for A4 photocopy paper.

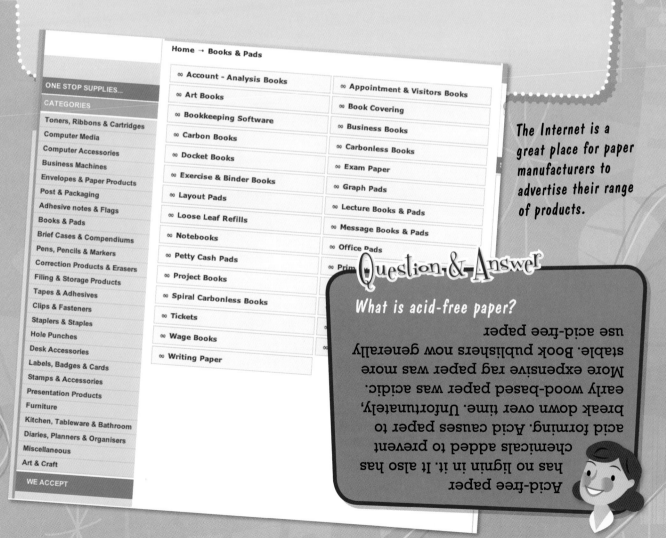

The Internet is a great place for paper manufacturers to advertise their range of products.

ONE STOP SUPPLIES...

CATEGORIES

Toners, Ribbons & Cartridges
Computer Media
Computer Accessories
Business Machines
Envelopes & Paper Products
Post & Packaging
Adhesive notes & Flags
Books & Pads
Brief Cases & Compendiums
Pens, Pencils & Markers
Correction Products & Erasers
Filing & Storage Products
Tapes & Adhesives
Clips & Fasteners
Staplers & Staples
Hole Punches
Desk Accessories
Labels, Badges & Cards
Stamps & Accessories
Presentation Products
Furniture
Kitchen, Tableware & Bathroom
Diaries, Planners & Organisers
Miscellaneous
Art & Craft

WE ACCEPT

Home → Books & Pads

∞ Account - Analysis Books
∞ Art Books
∞ Bookkeeping Software
∞ Carbon Books
∞ Docket Books
∞ Exercise & Binder Books
∞ Layout Pads
∞ Loose Leaf Refills
∞ Notebooks
∞ Petty Cash Pads
∞ Project Books
∞ Spiral Carbonless Books
∞ Tickets
∞ Wage Books
∞ Writing Paper

∞ Appointment & Visitors Books
∞ Book Covering
∞ Business Books
∞ Carbonless Books
∞ Exam Paper
∞ Graph Pads
∞ Lecture Books & Pads
∞ Message Books & Pads
∞ Office Pads

Question & Answer

What is acid-free paper?

Acid-free paper has no lignin in it. It also has chemicals added to prevent acid forming. Acid causes paper to break down over time. Unfortunately, early wood-based paper was acidic. More expensive rag paper was more stable. Book publishers now generally use acid-free paper.

Production of paper

Products may be made in factories in huge quantities. This is called mass production. They may also be made in small quantities by hand, by skilled craftspeople.

Mass production

Most paper is produced by machine. Machines make it possible to produce huge amounts of paper in all the different materials, sizes and qualities industries need. They have made paper cheap and identical, which is vital when it is used in other machines and processes. Huge newspaper presses, for instance, must be able to rely on newsprint of a certain quality.

The paper-making industry is, however, working hard to adapt to a rapidly changing world where communication is based on computers rather than paper. Demand for paper is still rising rapidly in China, India, Asia and Eastern Europe. Paper use is still a good way of judging the education and income of a society.

Machines like this one make it possible to produce the huge quantities of paper we use every day.

Question & Answer

What is the world's smallest newspaper?

The tiny micro journal *Vossa Senhoria* was first made in the 1930s by Brazil's Leonidas Schwindt. In 1985, his daughter made it even tinier. This newspaper has 16 pages and sells 5000 copies.

Small-scale production

Mass-produced paper is quite recent. Before this, all paper was made by hand in batches, rather than in continuous rolls by machines as it is made today.

Some paper is still made by hand. *Washi* or Japanese handmade paper is produced in an astounding variety, with all sorts of special inclusions, such as fibres of other plants and metallic flakes. One paper company says 'the soft, subtle textures and natural feeling of handmade paper is said to echo the warm heart of the papermaker who makes each sheet with devotion'.

People who buy this paper enjoy its unique qualities and variety. Handmade paper is used in crafts such as origami and other paper sculpture. People may also choose it for special letters, such as wedding invitations. You can even make paper at home from recycled paper or other materials.

A Chinese craftsman who specialises in handmade paper using traditional techniques stirs a vat of paper pulp.

Paper and the environment

Making any product affects the environment. It also affects the people who make the product. It is important to think about the impact of a product through its entire life cycle. This includes getting the raw materials, making the product and disposing of it. Any problems need to be worked on so products can be made in the best ways available.

Trees

Trees are essential to the health of our environment. In some places, the paper industry has been criticised for felling too many trees. This has destroyed animal homes, eroded the soil and caused water and air pollution. In other places, the paper industry plants trees in plantations faster than it cuts them down. In this way, paper can be made sustainably.

Replanting trees helps to make the paper industry's use of timber sustainable.

Pollution

The paper industry has been criticised for using so much energy and water, and creating pollution, especially in the bleaching process. The industry is working to lessen these problems. Today's paper-makers produce some unbleached paper and have developed less polluting bleaching methods.

This paper mill in Spain recycles used paper to produce new paper products.

Recycling

One of the most useful properties of paper is that it can be recycled into new paper. Recycling means some trees can be saved from harvesting, whether in natural forests or plantations.

The paper industry recycles paper to provide almost half its raw materials. Many households now recycle their paper, which is collected by waste companies. The paper is then sold back to paper manufacturers to be recycled as paper again.

Paper can usually be recycled four to seven times before the fibres become too short to mat together well. The recycled paper is pulped, cleaned, de-inked and fed into the cycle. It is usually mixed with fresh wood pulp to make paperboard, newsprint or toilet paper.

Question & Answer

What can you make with paper mâché?

In the 1800s, paper mâché was used to make fast, lightweight canoes and racing boats. You can recycle paper by making paper mâché masks and party piñatas filled with sweets. What else could you use paper mâché for?

29

Questions to think about

We need to conserve the raw materials used to produce even ordinary objects such as paper. Recycling resources such as metal, conserving energy and preventing pollution as much as possible means there will be enough resources in the future and a cleaner environment.

These are some questions you might like to think about:

❋ How many different uses for paper can you think of? What is the most unusual?

❋ What ingredients could you use from home or school to make some paper by hand?

❋ How can you recycle all the paper at school?

❋ Take apart a cardboard box from food packaging or a toy. How was it made?

❋ How many paper products made from recycled paper can you buy in the supermarket? Look at packaging in particular.

❋ How has electronic communication affected people's use of paper?

Paper is a wonderful craft medium which can be cut, folded, stamped, embossed and even curled.

Glossary

chalk
soft, white, powdery limestone made of fossil shells

chlorine
a poisonous chemical

distributors
shops or wholesalers that have the right to sell a particular product in a certain area

embossed
decorated with a raised pattern that has been pressed into the paper

export
send overseas to be sold

fibres
long strands (in paper, of cellulose) that can join with others

filtered
having the waste strained out

flexible
able to bend

hardwood trees
trees containing short fibres (1 millimetre long) such as eucalypt, acacia and birch

imported
brought into a country from overseas to be sold

kaolin
fine white clay

linen
cloth made from a certain plant fibre

manufacturers
makers, usually factories

opacity
not letting light through

pallets
portable platforms to store or move goods

paper mâché
hard material made of dried paper pulp and glue

paperboard
thick, strong, rigid paper material

petrochemical factories
factories that make chemical products, such as plastic, from petroleum oil

printing press
machine for printing books

slurry
a watery mass of pulp

softwood trees
conifer trees with long fibres (3 millimetres) such as pine, spruce and cedar

timber plantations
forests planted by people for harvesting timber

wholesalers
businesses that buy very large quantities of goods and sell them to shops, rather than directly to the consumer

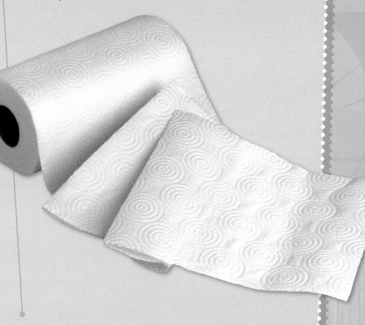

Index